Medical
Marvels

A CHAPTER BOOK

BY CATHERINE NICHOLS

children's press®

A Division of Scholastic Inc.
New York   Toronto   London   Auckland   Sydney
Mexico City   New Delhi   Hong Kong
Danbury, Connecticut

For Dean

ACKNOWLEDGMENTS

The author would like to thank all those who gave their time and knowledge to
help with this book. In particular, special thanks go to John Fleischman,
Ivan Yaeger, Abila Reyes, media specialist at the Children's Medical Center Dallas,
and the people at the Christopher Reeve Paralysis Foundation.

Library of Congress Cataloging-in-Publication Data

Nichols, Catherine.
  Medical marvels : a chapter book / By Catherine Nichols.
      p. cm. – (True tales)
  Includes bibliographical references and index.
  ISBN 0-516-23726-8 (lib. bdg.)   0-516-24686-0 (pbk.)
  1. Medical innovations—Juvenile literature.
  2. Medical technology—Juvenile literature.
  3. Medicine—Juvenile literature. I. Title II. Series.

R855.4.N535 2004
610'.28—dc22

                           2004005066

CONTENTS

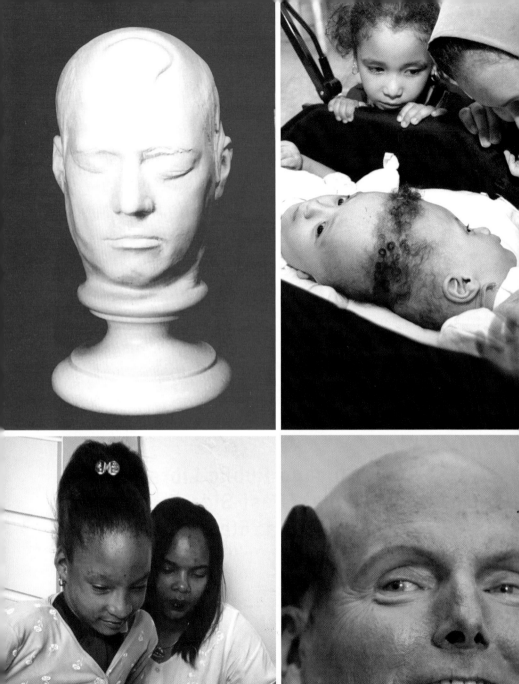

INTRODUCTION

Advances in medicine are going on all the time. Doctors and scientists are always looking for ways to help people who have become sick or injured.

In 1848, Phineas Gage was involved in a terrible accident. From his injury, doctors learned something about how the brain works.

Over the years, doctors continued to study the brain, and what they found out later helped Mohamed and Ahmed Ibrahim. These twin boys were born joined together at the head. Doctors separated them in a successful operation.

Medical advances helped Diamond Excell, too. Diamond was born without arms. Doctors fitted her with special arms that she controls with her chest and back muscles.

In 1995, actor Christopher Reeve was **paralyzed** (PAR-uh-lyzd) in an accident. At one time, doctors would have said that there was no hope for him. We now know that's not true. In the study of medicine, anything is possible.

CHAPTER ONE

THE MAN WITH A HOLE IN HIS HEAD

Phineas Gage left Cavendish, Vermont, on a cold winter's day in January, 1850. In his hand he carried a long iron rod. Phineas had been invited to speak at a medical college in Boston, Massachusetts. He had an incredible story to tell the doctors there. The iron rod was an important part of his story.

A plaster cast of Phineas Gage's head

Phineas spoke to doctors at Harvard University.

Two years earlier, Phineas had been involved in a terrible accident. At the time, Phineas was a foreman for a construction crew. The crew was blasting through mountain rock in order to lay down railroad lines. During one such blast, the iron rod shot through his head.

Doctor John Harlow reached Phineas an hour after the accident. He was amazed to find his patient awake and talking. After the doctor examined Phineas, he was even more amazed. By all rights, Phineas should not have been alive. The rod had gone in through his left cheek and passed through his brain. It left through the middle of his forehead, cracking his skull as it did so.

Doctor John Harlow

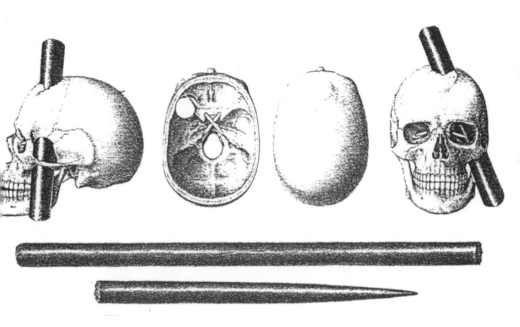

A diagram showing where the rod entered Phineas's skull

Doctor Harlow cleaned the wound. He carefully pressed two large pieces of bone back into place and closed the torn skin. Then he bandaged Phineas and put him to bed. Over the next two weeks, Phineas began to heal. Then **bacteria** (bak-TIHR-ee-uh) crept into the wound, and he developed an infection. Back in the mid 1800s, there were no **antibiotics** (an-ti-bye-OT-iks) to take. Phineas became very sick. He had high fevers. His wound oozed **pus**. Luckily for him, Doctor Harlow took very good care of him. After ten weeks, Phineas was fully recovered. Or was he?

Although Phineas's wounds had healed, his personality was no longer the same. Before the accident, Phineas had been a responsible young man. By all accounts, he had been a good foreman. After the accident, this was no longer true. Phineas returned to his job a changed man. He was rude and often insulted his crew. He couldn't stick to a decision, changing his mind again and again. Soon, he was fired from his job. Doctor Harlow was puzzled by the changes in Phineas.

Doctor Harlow wrote about Phineas's case in a medical journal. He did not mention Phineas's personality changes. Phineas was his patient, and doctors are required to respect their patients' privacy. The doctors in Boston had read Doctor Harlow's article and wanted to talk to Phineas. When Phineas met with the doctors, they did not know he had once been quite different. They examined him and made a plaster model of his head. They listened to his story.

Some of the doctors didn't believe Phineas. They thought he had made up his story and was faking his injuries. They thought it was impossible for anyone to survive an accident like the one he had described.

After leaving Boston, Phineas drifted from place to place. He found work caring for horses. Later, he accepted a job as a stagecoach driver in South America. Phineas now seemed to prefer working with animals.

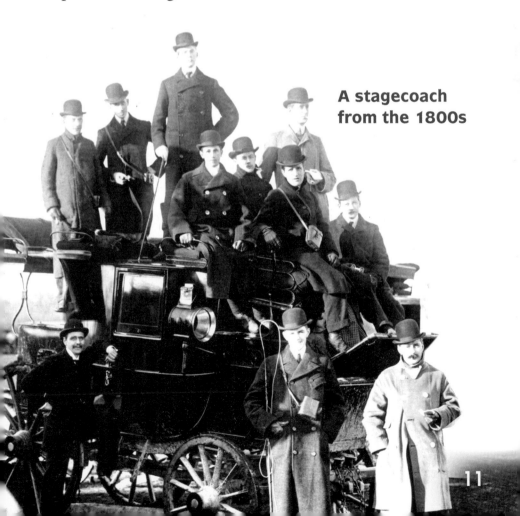

A stagecoach from the 1800s

When he was around people, he quarreled with them. His family and friends insisted he was no longer the Phineas Gage they once knew.

Why was this? How had the accident changed Phineas's personality? Today, doctors think they know the answer. The brain has different parts, and each part controls a specific activity. For instance, one part controls a person's ability to speak.

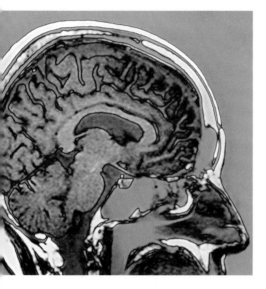

A side view of the brain

Another part controls the ability to understand language. In Phineas's case, the accident damaged his **frontal lobes**. This part of the brain controls a person's ability to make decisions and to get along with other people.

When this part of his brain was damaged, Phineas's behavior changed. He had trouble getting along with his friends and fellow workers. He could no longer make good decisions. Once, as a test, Doctor Harlow offered Phineas one thousand dollars for some worthless pebbles Phineas had collected. Phineas refused the deal.

Phineas lived in good health for eleven years after his accident. Then, while visiting his sister's family in San Francisco, he had a number of **seizures** (SEE-zhurs). As time

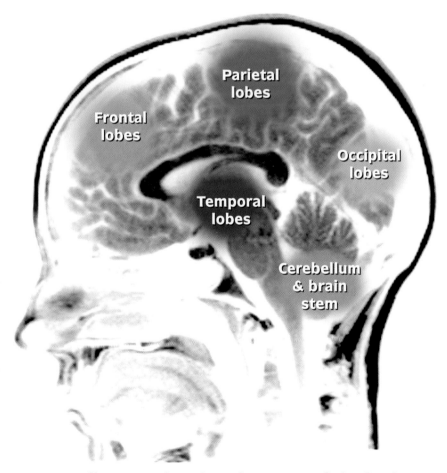

A diagram showing the parts of the brain

went on, the seizures got worse, and they came more often. Although the San Francisco doctors did not know what caused them, it's likely that his accident had something to do with the seizures. Whatever the cause, on May 21, 1860, Phineas Gage died and was buried in San Francisco. He was not quite thirty-seven years old.

Doctor Harlow didn't learn of Phineas's death for six years. As soon as he heard the news, he wrote to the family and asked if he could have Phineas's skull. He wanted to show it to the doctors in Boston who hadn't believed Phineas. The family agreed.

Phineas's body was dug up. An examination showed a crack the size of a quarter in his skull. Surrounding the crack were two large pieces of bone. Doctor Harlow had pushed these pieces back into place many years ago. New bone had grown around the edges. The skull was the final proof. Phineas had been telling the truth.

This memorial plaque to Phineas Gage
tells the story of his accident.

CHAPTER TWO

FACE-TO-FACE AT LAST

On October 11, 2003, nurses wheeled Mohamed and Ahmed Ibrahim into an operating room. The two-year-old twin boys entered on a single **gurney**. When they were wheeled out, each boy had his own separate one.

Mohamed and Ahmed Ibrahim

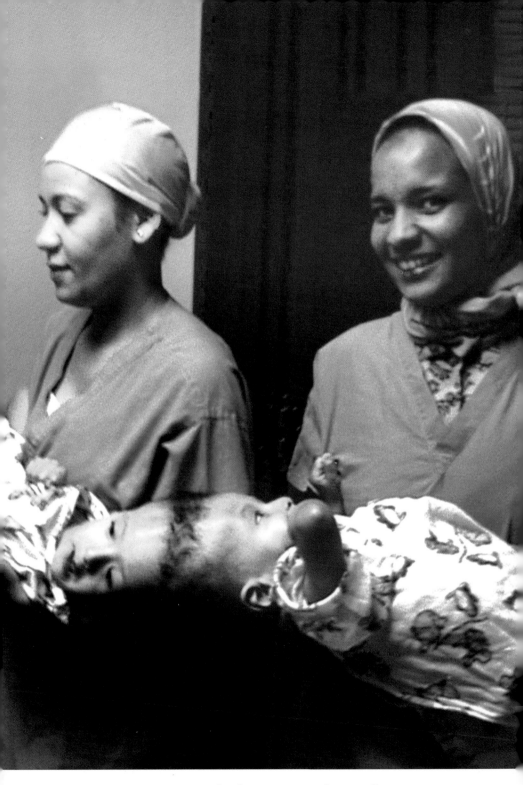

Two nurses are needed to carry the twins.

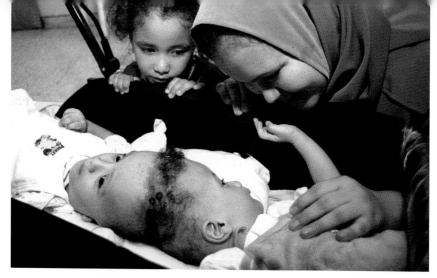

Ahmed reaches out to touch his mother's face.

Mohamed and Ahmed were born joined at the head. The only way they could be separated was through surgery. **Conjoined twins** are very rare. They happen just one out of 200,000 births. Twins joined at the head are even rarer. This happens just once in every 1.5 million births.

How do twins become conjoined? In the **womb** (WOOM), an **embryo** (EM-bree-oh) begins to split into identical twins, but stops part way. The embryo continues to develop as twins. When the babies are born, they are fused together.

Mohamed and Ahmed were born in Egypt on June 2, 2001. From the start, the two boys had very different personalities. Mohamed is the outgoing twin. Ahmed is quieter. At first, the boys needed special care, so they stayed in a hospital. Their parents didn't want their sons in a hospital for their entire lives. They wanted the boys separated. Separating the twins was risky, though.

Luckily, doctors at the Children's Medical Center in Dallas, Texas, heard about the twins. They agreed to try to separate them. First, though, the doctors had to discover if

A doctor looks at brain scans of the twins.

the boys shared a brain. If they did, then separation would be impossible. Tests showed that the boys had separate brains, although they did share some **veins**. These veins would make the operation especially difficult.

Before they could operate, the doctors needed to prepare. They talked to other doctors who had separated conjoined twins. They made detailed models of the boys' brains and skull. They **rehearsed** what each member of the team would do in the operating room.

The boys also needed to prepare. They needed to be strong enough to withstand

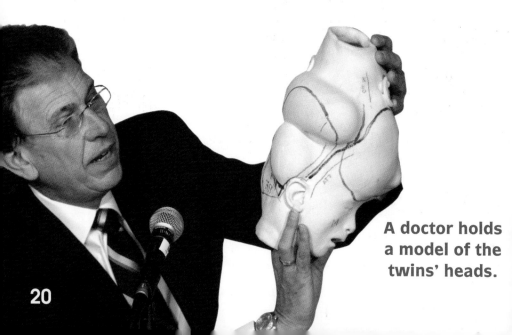

A doctor holds a model of the twins' heads.

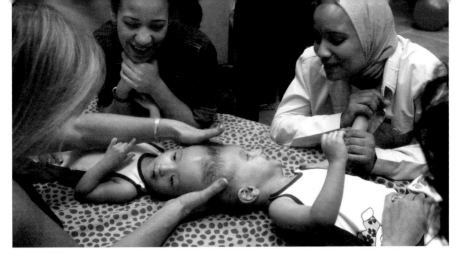

A physical therapist massages the twins.

the operation. Since birth, they had spent every moment on their backs. Most children their age were walking. Mohamed and Ahmed couldn't walk, but they could strengthen their muscles. After working with a **physical therapist** (FIZ-uh-kuhl THER-uh-pist), the boys were soon able to scoot and roll their way around a room.

The next step was to stretch the skin around the boys' skull. After the boys were separated, the doctors would need extra skin to cover their skulls. To do this, tiny balloons were placed underneath the skin. Each day, a mixture of salty water was added to the balloons. As the balloons expanded, the skin stretched.

Finally, the boys were ready to be separated. The operation lasted thirty-three hours. Afterward, the boys were given drugs to put them in a **coma** (KOH-muh). This was to prevent their brains from swelling. At their bedsides, their parents, doctors, and nurses waited for them to wake up.

The medical team has been pleased with the twins' recovery. Each day they have gotten stronger. Soon, they will be ready for the next step. In the months to come, the boys will need more operations. Above their foreheads, they have no skulls. Doctors will have to **reconstruct** them. For now, the boys must wear helmets to protect their brains.

Almost two weeks after their operation, the boys had a special surprise. Mohamed was wheeled into Ahmed's hospital room. There, for the first time since they were born, the brothers saw each other face-to-face.

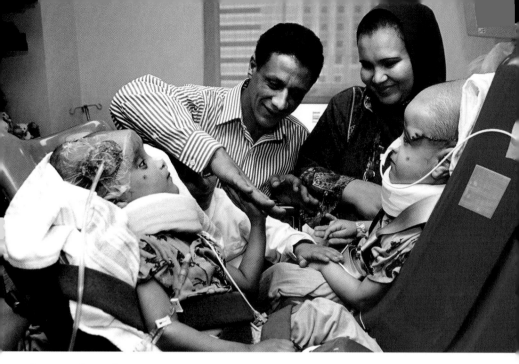

Mohamed (left) and Ahmed (right) meet for the first time.

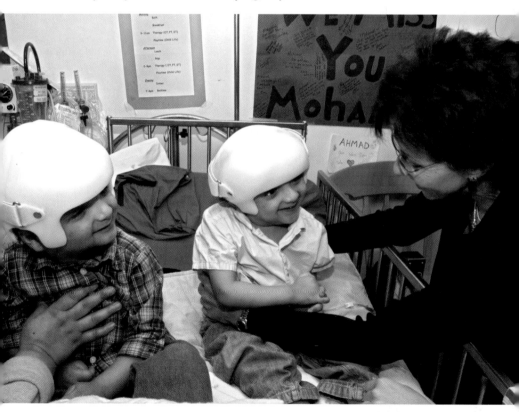

Mohamed (left) and Ahmed (right) wear
special helmets to protect their brains.

CHAPTER THREE

ARMS ARE FOR HUGGING

The first time Diamond Excell hugged her mother she was eleven years old. It wasn't that Diamond didn't want to hug her before then. She just wasn't able to. Diamond was born without shoulders or arms. She has **Robert's Syndrome**, a very rare birth condition.

Diamond Excell

Diamond uses her foot to pick up objects.

Diamond eating with her feet

Being without arms didn't stop Diamond from doing most of the things she wanted. She ate, wrote, and brushed her teeth all by herself. Instead of using hands, though, Diamond used her feet.

How did Diamond finally get to hug her mother? She has inventor Ivan Yaeger to thank for that. Ivan made Diamond a pair of artificial arms. Diamond's new arms are not like ordinary **prosthetics**. They are electronic.

Ivan Yaeger holding parts from his invention

With her arms, Diamond can grasp things by moving her finger and thumb together. Her wrists can turn, and her arms can go up and down. When she walks, her arms swing naturally by her sides.

In a way, Ivan had been working on these arms since he was in junior high school. That's when he first designed an artificial arm for a science fair project. Back in the seventh grade, Ivan's favorite television show was *The Six Million Dollar Man*. The show was about a **bionic** man, so Ivan decided to make an electronic body part for his project.

Lee Majors played the part of the Six Million Dollar Man.

Diamond with Ivan

Ivan built an improved arm while in high school. A few years later, he received a **patent** for this arm. He used this design to create Diamond's arms. Next, Ivan worked with Eugene Silva, a **prosthetist** (proz-THET-ist), to build and test the arms.

Each arm has three **joints**. Motors open and close them. To open a joint, Diamond twitches a back muscle. To close one, she flexes her chest muscles. For the first few weeks after she got her new arms, Diamond had to have special training to learn how to control them.

Except for the hands, the arms are covered with stocking-net material. Underneath this material is padding to protect the electronics and cable wires inside. Once Diamond has learned how to fully operate her arms, they will be refitted with more lifelike covering.

Diamond tries out her new arms while using a computer.

The hands look like real hands, though. That's because one of Diamond's cousins allowed her hand to be used as a model. The hands are covered with latex, a kind of plastic. Their color matches Diamond's natural skin tone.

As Diamond grows, the arms will need to be lengthened. However, the electronics that allow the arms to move have to be replaced only every five years or so.

For now, Diamond is very happy with her new arms. So is her mother, Delia. After getting her first hug from her daughter, Delia said, "It felt so good. Words can't even express the way I felt when she hugged me with those arms."

Diamond gets a kiss from her mother.

CHAPTER FOUR

A SUPERMAN

In November 2000, Christopher Reeve did something remarkable. He raised the tip of his index finger on his left hand. What was so special about lifting a finger? Christopher Reeve is a **quadriplegic**. He has been in a wheelchair since 1995. That was the year Christopher had a terrible accident.

Christopher Reeve

Christopher Reeve played the part of
Superman in the 1978 movie.

Even experienced riders can be injured when riding a horse

While riding in a competition, his horse stopped suddenly. Christopher was thrown headfirst to the ground, breaking his neck.

In the hospital, doctors told him the bad news. He was paralyzed. That meant he was unable to move. He could not feel anything below his neck. In order to breathe, he had to use a **ventilator**. The worst news of all was that he would never get better.

Christopher did not accept this. Before the accident, he was a very active man. As an actor, he often performed his own stunts. In 1978, he played the part of Superman. In that movie, Christopher pretended he had superhuman powers. In real life, though, Christopher didn't have special powers to help him. He had only his determination to help him get better.

When he fell from his horse, Christopher damaged his **spinal cord**. Your spinal cord runs along the length of your back. In your spinal cord are millions of **nerves**. These nerves send messages between the brain and the rest of your body.

In Christopher's case, nerve cells in his spinal cord had died off. Without these cells, his spinal cord could not work properly. Messages from his brain were not getting through to the rest of his body.

Until recently, scientists thought that once the spinal cord was damaged, it was damaged forever. People with spinal cord injuries were helped to do what they could, but they were not expected to recover completely. Today, that thinking has changed. Research has shown that moving the body helps damaged nerve cells to relearn their jobs.

Five years after his accident, Christopher found out about a **rehabilitation** program that helps people with spinal cord injuries. The program is very demanding. Christopher has to do a lot of exercises. Three times a week he pedals a special exercise bike. Through a computer program, the bike sends out electrical pulses to leg muscles. The pulses cause the muscles to contract. This allows people who can't move their legs on their own to pedal the bike.

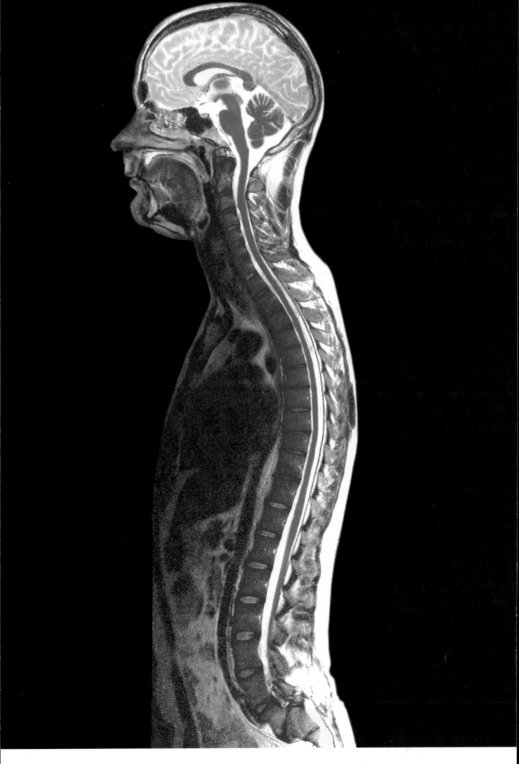

A body scan showing the brain (pink) and spinal cord (blue)

A patient pedals a special bicycle.

At first, Christopher could pedal for only five minutes. As his muscles became stronger, he could pedal for longer periods of time. Today, he rides his bike for thirty minutes or more at a time.

Christopher also works out in a pool. He pushes off the side of the pool with his legs and moves his arms. The water holds him up and makes it easier for him to move. It is relaxing, too. Christopher practices in the pool once a week for two hours.

Since beginning his exercise program, Christopher has made steady progress. One day, he realized he could feel his wife Dana's touch. Next, he was able to move his index finger. Today, he can wiggle his toes, move his

Dana and Christopher

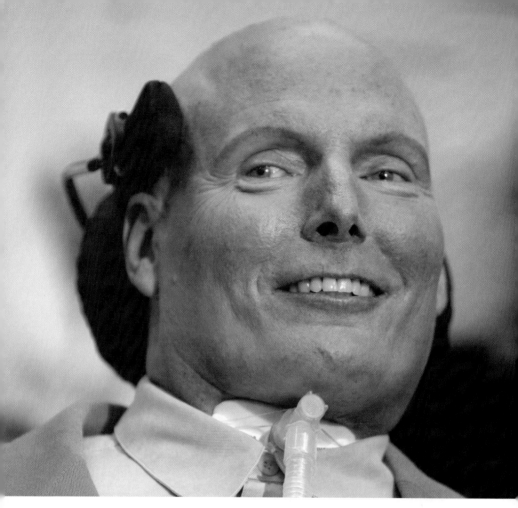

A ventilator in his neck helps Christopher breathe.

fingers, and feel the difference between something that is hot and something that is cold. He is also able to breathe without the ventilator for long periods of time.

There are other benefits, too. Studies have shown that paralyzed people who exercise have fewer pressure sores, **blood clots**, and infections. Before beginning this program, Christopher often had to go into the hospital. Since he began the program, he has not been in the hospital once.

His doctor, John McDonald, is impressed with Christopher's progress. He said that "no one who has suffered an injury as severe as Chris's has regained the amount of motor and sensory function he has—not even close."

John McDonald

**Christopher is head of the
Christopher Reeve Paralysis Foundation.**

Christopher Reeve doesn't only want to help himself. He wants to help other people with spinal cord injuries. To do this, he started the Christopher Reeve Paralysis Foundation. Each year the foundation gives away millions of dollars to scientists to do more research.

Christopher knows that he still has a long way to go. He is determined to keep trying. He has said that "One day, I expect to get up from this wheelchair." If anyone can, it will be Christopher Reeve. He is truly a superman!

Christopher Reeve speaking at the 1996 Democratic National Convention

GLOSSARY

antibiotic (an-ti-bye-OT-ik) a drug used to fight infections

bacteria (bak-TIHR-ee-uh) tiny living things that sometimes cause illness

bionic dealing with mechanical parts that replace body parts

blood clot a mass of blood that has gelled

coma (KOH-muh) an unconscious state

conjoined twins twins born with their bodies joined at some point

embryo (EM-bree-oh) the form of an animal as it grows before birth

frontal lobes the front part of the brain that lies behind the forehead

gurney a metal stretcher with wheels

joint a place where parts or objects are joined together

nerve one of the fibers that carry messages between the brain and other parts of the body

paralyzed (PAR-uh-lyzd) to have lost feeling or movement in the body

patent a legal document giving an inventor sole rights to his/her invention

physical therapist (FIZ-uh-kuhl THER-uh-pist) a person who treats injuries with exercise

prosthetic (proz-THET-ik) a replacement for a body part

prosthetist (proz-THET-ist) someone who is an expert in body part replacements

pus a thick yellowish liquid that comes out of an infected wound

quadriplegic someone unable to use his or her arms and legs

reconstruct to remake something that has been damaged or destroyed

rehabilitation the act of making someone healthy again

rehearse to practice for a later event

Robert's Syndrome a rare condition that involves loss of limb bones

seizure (SEE-zhur) a fit in which muscles contract suddenly and with great force

spinal cord a bundle of nerves that carries messages between the brain and the rest of the body

vein a tube that carries blood to the heart

ventilator a machine that helps a person breathe

womb (WOOM) the part of a female's body that carries an unborn child

FIND OUT MORE

The Man With a Hole in His Head

www.deakin.edu.au/hbs/GAGEPAGE

Everything you want to know about Phineas Gage can be found on this Web site.

Face-to-Face at Last

www.dallasnews.com/sharedcontent/dws/spe/2003/twins/

See photos of Ahmed and Mohamed and read about their progress.

Arms Are for Hugging

www.yaegerco.com/tyf_tyc.html

Read more about Ivan Yaeger, the inventor of Diamond's artificial arm.

A Superman

www.apacure.com

This Web site for the Christopher Reeve Paralysis Foundation has information on spinal cord injuries, as well as the latest research.

More Books to Read

Being Paralyzed by Linda O'Neill, Rourke Publishing, 2001

Joined at Birth: The Lives of Conjoined Twins by Elaine Landau, Franklin Watts, 1997

The Making of My Special Hand: Madison's Story by Jamee Riggio Heelan, Peachtree Publishers, 2000

Phineas Gage: A Gruesome but True Story About Brain Science by John Fleischman, Houghton Mifflin, 2002

INDEX

PHOTO CREDITS

MEET THE AUTHOR

 Catherine Nichols has worked in children's publishing as an editor, project manager, and author. She has written many children's nonfiction books, from sports biographies to science books about endangered habitats. She lives in Jersey City, New Jersey, with her teenage daughter.